Hippo or Rhino?
A Compare and Contrast Book

by Samantha Collison

Hippos, short for hippopotamuses, and rhinos, short for rhinoceroses, are both mammals, like us.

There are two species of hippos: the common (or river) and the pygmy hippo.

common hippo

pygmy hippo

There are five living species of rhinos.

White and black rhinos are native to Africa.

The Indian, Javan, and Sumatran rhinos are native to Southern Asia.

white rhino

black rhino

Indian rhino

Javan rhino

Sumatran rhino

Hippos spend most of their time in or near lakes, pools, mudholes, or rivers. They are sometimes called "river horses."

Hippos cannot swim so they gallop or bounce along the bottom of the water!

Rhinos in Africa spend most of their time in the grasslands. Asian rhinos spend most of their time in wetlands and rainforests.

Because they spend so much time in the water, hippos have body parts (adaptations) to help them in the water.

They have clear membranes to protect their open eyes underwater—like we might use goggles to see underwater.

They can close their nostrils and hold their breath for over five minutes!

Their eyes and ears are on top of their heads so they can see above the water surface even when sitting in the water.

Black rhinos use their upper lips to grab and hold onto things (prehensile) much like we use our fingers.

black rhino

All rhinos have one or two horns made from keratin—like our fingernails and hair. The horns will grow back if they are worn down or broken. They use their horns to dig for food, break branches, or to defend themselves.

The three Asian rhino species have tusks and use these large incisors (teeth) to fight as their horns aren't as large as their African relatives.

Indian rhino

Hippos sweat a red mucus to keep their skin moist. The mucus also acts as a natural sunscreen to protect their skin.

Rhinos soak in mud or roll around in dust to protect their skin from sunburn and insect bites.

Like all mammals both hippos and rhinos have some hair or fur. Hippos have stiff whiskers on their upper lips and fuzzy hair around their ears and tails.

Rhinos have hair around their ears and tails.

Both hippos and rhinos eat plants. They are herbivores.

Hippos eat short grasses near the water and fruit that's fallen to the ground. They spend most of their days wallowing in shallow water. They can spend up to six hours a day grazing grasses near the water.

Hippos' teeth are constantly growing. Their incisors (tusks) can grow up to 20 inches (51 cm) and are used to fight off other hippos and scare enemies.

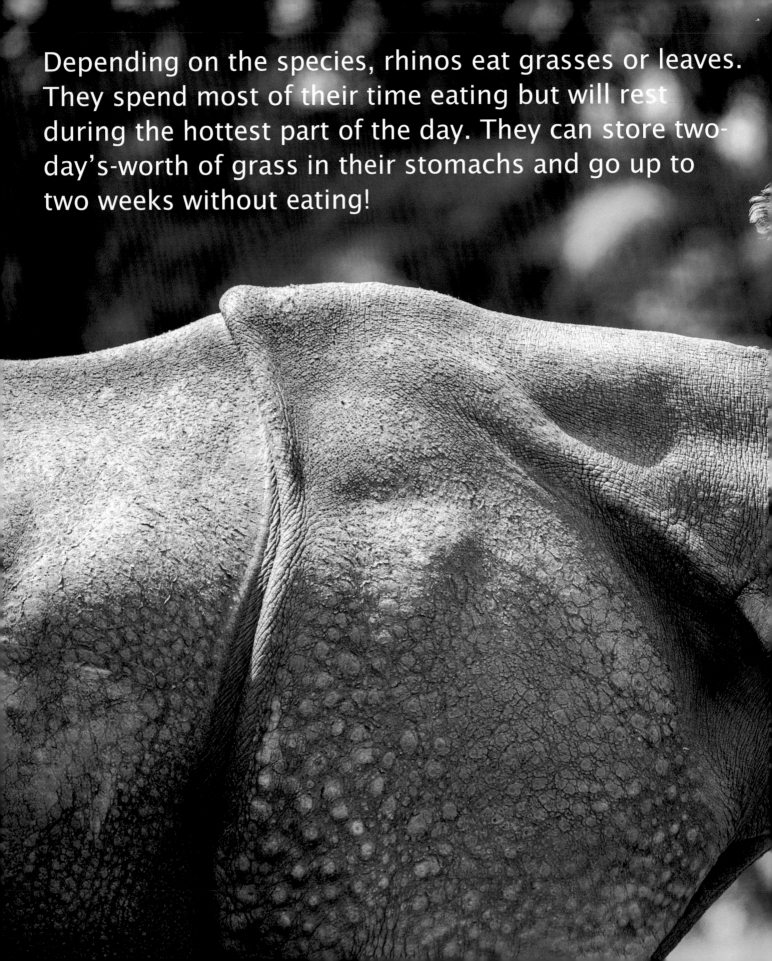

Depending on the species, rhinos eat grasses or leaves. They spend most of their time eating but will rest during the hottest part of the day. They can store two-day's-worth of grass in their stomachs and go up to two weeks without eating!

Their molar teeth
are great for
grinding vegetation.

A hippo herd is sometimes called a bloat, pod, or siege. The herd can have 10 to 30 members with one dominant male.

A rhino herd is sometimes called a crash. The small herds are mostly males. Dominant males (bulls) spend most of their time claiming their territories with dung and urine. Females do not have territories but move through male territories.

Hippos are vulnerable to habitat loss and being hunted for their ivory (large incisors called tusks). Hippos were once common in all of Africa but are now mostly found in East Africa.

Rhinos are critically endangered due to poaching. Although it has no healing properties, rhino horn has been used in traditional Asian medicine to treat a variety of ailments.

Rhinos were once found in all of Africa and Asia. Depending on the species, they can now only be found in Borneo & Sumatra, Namibia, the Eastern Himalayas, and coastal East Africa.

Zoos and conservation organizations across the world are helping these animals.

For Creative Minds

Thinking it Through

Rhinos were once found all across Africa and Asia. They are now only found in Borneo and Sumatra, Namibia, eastern Himalayas, and coastal east Africa. Can you find those locations on a map or a globe?

If hippo and rhino babies are called "calves" and the dads are called "bulls," what do you think the moms are called? Why?

Black rhinos use their upper lips to grab and hold onto things (prehensile) much like we use our fingers. What other animals can you think of that use prehensile body parts to grab and hold onto things?

Hippos and rhinos are mammals, just like us. Can you see hair or whiskers on any of the photos? Most of us have hair on our heads. Where else do you have hair on your body? What other characteristics do mammals share?

Look back through the pictures and see how many photos of hippos you see with the red mucous showing.

A hippo's adaptations allow it to have most of its body underwater with just its eyes, ears, and nose above water. Can you think of any other animals that have similar adaptations?

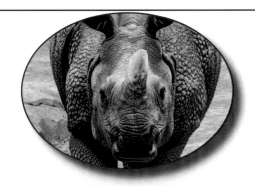

Hippo or Rhino?

Hippos spend most of their time in the water. They have a clear eyelid to help them keep eyes open underwater.

Hippos' eyes and ears are on top of their heads so they can see when sitting in water.

Hippos have a red mucus to protect their skin from sunburn.

Black rhinos use their upper lip to grab and hold onto things.

Depending on the species, rhinos spend most of their time in grasslands, wetlands, or rainforests.

Rhinos have one or two horns.

Answers: hippos: 2, 4, 6 rhinos: 1, 3, 5

True or False?

Using what you read in the book, determine whether these statements are true or false.

1 Both hippos and rhinos only live in Africa.	**2** Hippos and rhinos are mammals, so they have some hair on parts of their bodies.
3 Hippos spend most of their time in the water and rhinos spend most of their time on land.	**4** Hippos can hold their breath underwater for up to 5 minutes!
5 All rhinos use their upper lips to grab and hold onto things (prehensile).	**6** All rhinos have one or two horns that they use to dig for food or to protect themselves.
7 Rhinos sweat a red mucus that acts as a natural sunscreen to protect them from sunburns.	**8** Both hippos and rhinos eat fish and small mammals.

Answers: 1: False-rhinos also live in Asia. 2: True. 3: True. 4: True. 5: False-only black rhinos have this adaptation. 6: True. 7: False-hippos do but not rhinos. 8: False-they both eat grass.

Fun Facts

Swimming

Hippos spend most of their time in the water, but they can't swim—they gallop or bounce along the river bottom. Rhinos spend most of their time on land, but they are good swimmers.

Helping their ecosystems

After eating lots of grasses, hippos return to the water where they poop. Many fish and plankton rely on hippo poop for their food.

Many small land animals also rely on eating rhino poop. Rhino poop also helps disperse seeds.

Running

Hippos can run up to 14 mph on land and rhinos can run up to 40 mph.

How fast can you run?

Eating

Hippos can store two-days' worth of grass in their stomachs and can go up to two weeks without eating.

Babies

Hippo moms give birth to a single calf that can weigh between 50 to 110 pounds (23 to 50 kg). Calves nurse about 8 months and can even nurse underwater.

Rhino moms usually give birth to one calf but sometimes have two. The calves weigh between 88 to 140 pounds (40 to 63 kg).

Related to?

The closest relatives to hippos are pigs, whales, and dolphins!

The closest relatives to rhinos are tapis, horses, and zebras.

Size

Hippos and white rhinos are both about six feet (1.8 meters) high at the shoulders. A Sumatran rhino is only 4.8 feet (145 centimeters).

How tall are you?

Eyesight

Rhinos have poor eyesight and sometimes charge boulders or trees.

This book is dedicated to my two curious nieces, Norah and Charlotte—the world's number one hippo and rhino fans! —SC

Thanks to Jay Ballard, Guest Services Supervisor - Volunteer Services at the San Diego Zoo Wildlife Alliance for verifying the information in this book.

All photographs are licensed through Adobe Stock Photos or Shutterstock.

Library of Congress Cataloging-in-Publication Data

Names: Collison, Samantha, 1983- author.
Title: Hippo or rhino? : a compare and contrast book / by Samantha
    Collison.
Description: Mt. Pleasant, SC : Arbordale Publishing, LLC, [2023] |
    Includes bibliographical references.
Identifiers: LCCN 2022036978 (print) | LCCN 2022036979 (ebook) | ISBN
    9781643519913 (paperback) | ISBN 9781638170105 (interactive
    dual-language, read along) | ISBN 9781638170488 (epub) | ISBN
    9781638170297 (adobe pdf)
Subjects: LCSH: Hippopotamidae--Juvenile literature. |
    Rhinoceroses--Juvenile literature.
Classification: LCC QL737.U57 C67 2023 (print) | LCC QL737.U57 (ebook) |
    DDC 599.63/5--dc23/eng/20220803
LC record available at https://lccn.loc.gov/2022036978
LC ebook record available at https://lccn.loc.gov/2022036979

Translated into Spanish: *¿Hipopótamo o rinoceronte? Un libro de comparaciones y contrastes*
Spanish paperback ISBN: 9781638172932
Spanish ePub ISBN: 9781638173052
Spanish PDF ebook ISBN: 9781638173014
Dual-language read-along available online at www.fathomreads.com

English Lexile® Level: 930L

Bibliography

"Asian Rhinos." Wwf.panda.org, wwf.panda.org/discover/knowledge_hub/endangered_species/rhinoceros/
    asian_rhinos/.
"Hippo | San Diego Zoo Animals & Plants." Sandiegozoo.org, 2009, animals.sandiegozoo.org/animals/hippo.
"Hippopotamus | Nature | PBS." Nature, www.pbs.org/wnet/nature/group/mammals/hippopotamus-mammals/.

Printed in the US
This product conforms to CPSIA 2008

Arbordale Publishing
Mt. Pleasant, SC 29464
www.ArbordalePublishing.com